The Lady with the Lamp

Written by
Jill Atkins

Illustrated by
Heike Jane Zimmermann

Have you or your family ever been sick and needed to go to hospital?

If you have, you will know that nurses work hard and hospitals are kept clean.

It was not always like this, but one lady helped to change things.

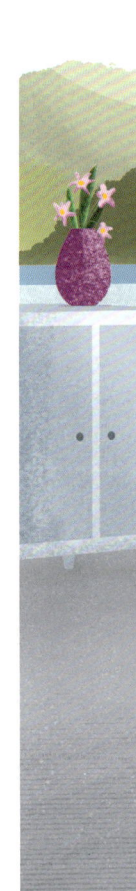

When Florence Nightingale was a little girl, her father didn't allow his daughters to go to school.

Florence and her sister were taught at home. They learned a lot about the world.

The Nightingale family was rich. They had servants, as well as one house for the summer and one house for the winter.

So Florence didn't ever need to work to earn money.

Florence always wanted to look after sick people. But her father told her that rich girls didn't need to work.

He thought that nursing was the worst job for a girl. He thought that hospitals were dirty places where sick people died.

"Your place is in the home," he said. "My daughters will learn about finding a husband and being a good wife and mother."

Florence did not want to hear this! She wanted to help people.

Florence pleaded with her father.

In the end, Mr Nightingale could tell that she was earnest about it.

So he allowed Florence to go to Germany.

In Germany she learned about nursing and how to care for sick people.

She also learned how important it was to keep hospitals clean.

After that, Florence ran a hospital near her home for a few years.

Then she heard about fighting in a land on the coast of the Black Sea. Many troops were getting killed.

Word spread that too many troops were dying because there was nobody to care for them.

So Florence travelled to the fighting zone to help.

She found that the hospital was even worse than she had heard!

There were blocked drains, broken toilets and rats everywhere!

And the smell was disgusting!

It was Florence Nightingale to the rescue!

She and her team of nurses set to work. They cleaned it all and set up a hospital kitchen, so that the troops had better food.

It was worth it because fewer men died.

Florence kept an eye on the troops at night, walking around with her oil lamp.

So the troops called her "The Lady with the Lamp".

When the fighting was over, Florence returned home.

But she kept trying to make things better for fighting troops. She set up a training school for nurses and even met the queen!

Today Florence Nightingale is remembered as the founder of modern nursing.